MAGIC CASTLE READERS®

Butterfly Express

A book about life cycles

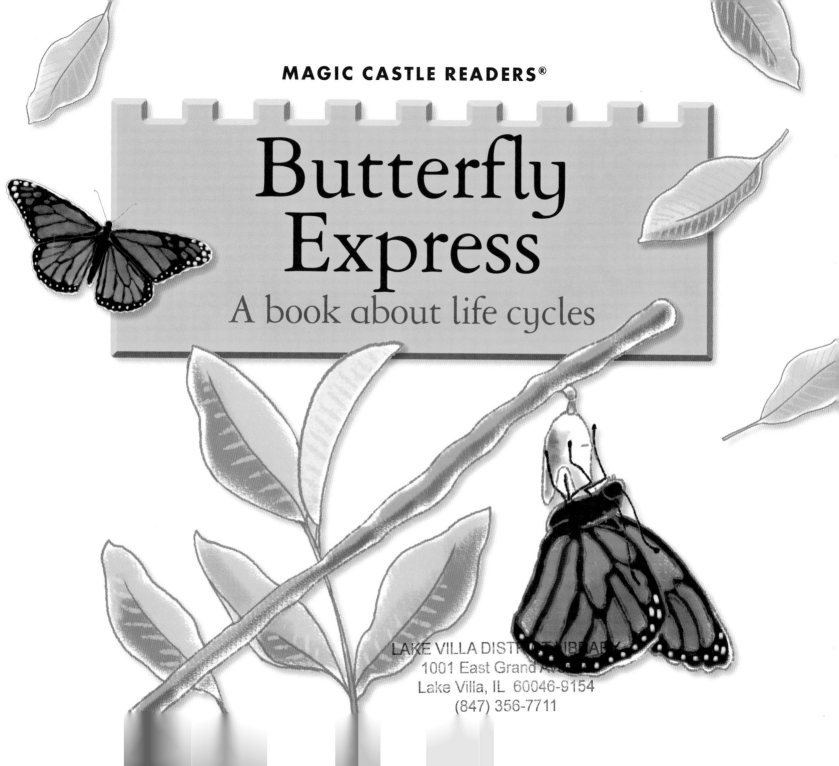

The Child's World

Published by The Child's World®
1980 Lookout Drive • Mankato, MN 56003-1705
800-599-READ • www.childsworld.com

Acknowledgments
The Child's World®: Mary Berendes, Publishing Director
The Design Lab: Design
Jody Jensen Shaffer: Editing

ISBN 9781623235888
LCCN 2013931419

Printed in the United States of America
Mankato, MN
July 2013
PA02177

Did you know...

A library is a magic castle with many Word Windows in it?

What is a Word Window?

If you said, "A book," you're right!

A book is a Word Window because the words and pictures let you look and see many things. Books are your windows to the wide, wide world around you.

The Library
Is a Magic Castle

Come to the Magic Castle
When you are growing tall.
Rows and rows of Word Windows
Line every single wall.
They reach up high,
As high as the sky,
And you'll want to open them all.
For every time you open one,
A new adventure has begun.

Anna opened a Word Window.
Here is what she read:

A little girl found a caterpillar in a field.
It was all alone.

The girl put her hand down near the caterpillar.
It climbed up one finger and down the other.

"I will take you home with me," said the girl.
And she did.

Her father made a cage for the caterpillar.
He used two pie pans and some wire.

The little girl put leaves and a stick in the cage.

The girl put the cage in a sunny window.

Every day the caterpillar ate leaves.
Every day it grew bigger.

One day, the caterpillar wiggled out of its skin.
Its new skin fit just right.

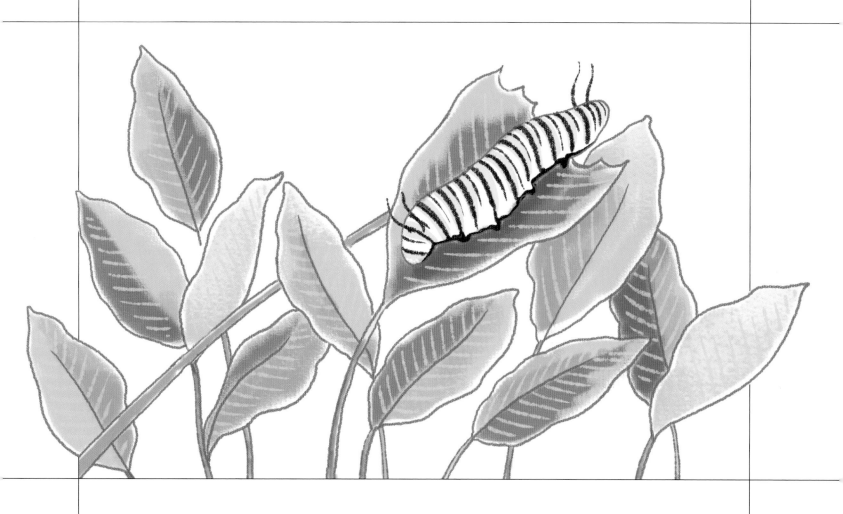

A few days later, the same thing happened.
Each time the caterpillar wiggled out of its
old skin, it was bigger.

Then one day, it climbed up on the stick.
The caterpillar made a tiny button of silk.

The caterpillar hung upside down from the silk.

The caterpillar wiggled out of its skin
for the last time. But this time, there was
a green shell underneath the old skin.

"When your caterpillar comes out of its shell,
it will not be a caterpillar at all," said the
girl's mother.

"What will it be?" asked the girl.
"You must wait and see," said her mother.

So the little girl waited.

The little girl wished she could see what was happening inside the shell. But she could not.

She waited and watched. Finally, one day,
she peeked in the cage and saw a surprise.

A beautiful butterfly sat where the caterpillar had been. The caterpillar had changed into a butterfly while it was inside the shell.

"How pretty," said the little girl.
Then she looked outside the window.
There was another surprise—snow!

"This is not good," said her father. "The snow is covering the flowers. The butterfly must drink nectar from the flowers or it will die."

"What can we do?" asked the little girl.
"I know where flowers grow in the wintertime,"
    said her father. "In California."

The girl's father called a friend
who was an airplane pilot.

"Yes," said the pilot. "I am flying to California today. I will take the butterfly with me."

The little girl put her butterfly in a box.
She made tiny holes in the box.
She wrote "Butterfly Express" on top.

The pilot took the butterfly with her
all the way to California.

There, she opened the box.
The butterfly flew away.
It found a field full of California flowers.

What a lucky butterfly!

Questions and Activities

(Write your answers on a sheet of paper.)

1. Name two things you learned about a butterfly's life.
   What else would you like to know?

2. Look at the picture on page 16.
   What does it show you about a butterfly's shell?

3. Did this story have any words you don't know?
   How can you find out what they mean?

4. Why did the little girl send the butterfly to California?
   Why could the butterfly not stay in the snow?

5. Did parts of this story make you feel sad or happy? Why?